DESTINATION
Central Coast

MAGNIFICENT PANORAMIC VIEWS

PANOGRAPHS
PUBLISHING PTY LTD

Shaped by water over countless centuries, the New South Wales Central Coast is today a vibrant mix of settled communities and magnificent natural scenery. Forested hills and rural enclaves give way to large inlets, lakes and lagoons, and to the fabulous stretch of rugged headlands and sparkling beaches that have made the Central Coast so popular. Its location – just an hour north of Sydney – means that the region attracts plenty of visitors, adding to its perennial holiday-like charm. There are countless bed-and-breakfasts and holiday houses, galleries and cafés, and an abundance of outdoor leisure opportunities.

In spite of its popularity, the Central Coast is still able to boast a wonderful variety of out-of-the-way locations. There are hidden beaches and little-visited bays, sprawling national parks and half-forgotten country roads. There are the massive Tuggerah Lakes and the seemingly endless coves of Brisbane Water. In fact, you never have far to travel before gazing out upon the magnificence of nature.

For many years, the Central Coast has been the chosen home of world-renowned landscape photographer Ken Duncan. In this wonderful mini volume, he turns his lens towards many of the region's most beautiful scenes. From Pearl Beach in the south to Norah Head in the north, Ken Duncan's panoramas capture a coastal wonderland glowing with spectacular colour and light.

Love is the immortal flow of energy that nourishes, extends and preserves. Its eternal goal is life.

Located not far from the main expressway to Sydney, Somersby Falls provides a delightful haven away from life's rush. Spring fed, the falls are constantly flowing. After rain, the waters thunder down the rock-face, reminding visitors of nature's spectacular power.

TITLE PAGE
Harmony, Brisbane Waters, NSW

PREVIOUS PAGE
Terrigal Beach, NSW

THIS PAGE
Somersby Falls, NSW

ELVIS PRESLEY

Truth is like the sun.
You can shut it out
for a time,
but it ain't going away.

Sunset at Avoca Beach reveals a bare expanse
of sand and surf and a rock-walled paddling pool
for the kids. This beach is crowded during summer,
but in the cooler months (as in this photo)
it is often wonderfully desolate.

THIS PAGE
Avoca Beach, NSW

NEXT PAGE
Ettalong aerial, NSW

It's a beautiful day,
don't let it get away.

This is one of Ken's favourite Central Coast scenes:
a local wharf with traditional clinker-built boats
and a vast, mirror-like lake disappearing softly
in the distance. Here, visitors can hire a boat
and while away a few hours fishing.

Tuggerah Lakes, The Entrance, NSW

SAMUEL JOHNSON

*Great works
are performed
not by strength
but by perseverance.*

*Captured from the craggy sandstone heights
of Mount Ettalong Lookout, this view of Pearl Beach
looks south towards Sydney across a gloriously blue
Broken Bay. Lion Island crouches in the centre;
to its right lies the opening
of the mighty Hawkesbury River.*

THIS PAGE
Pearl Beach, NSW

NEXT PAGE
Dawning of a New Day, Wamberal, NSW

There is more to life than increasing its speed.

Fishermen love this famous channel at The Entrance where the massive Tuggerah Lakes system joins the open sea. This view captures something of the town's idyllic holiday feel. The pace of life is slower and there's a chance of a big catch!

PREVIOUS PAGE
The Entrance aerial, NSW

THIS PAGE
Drifting Tides, The Entrance, NSW

*Simplicity is
the ultimate
sophistication.*

*Like an invitation to adventure, this long timber jetty
beckons viewers into the sunset. A lone yacht
at the jetty's end reinforces the imagery of escape:
Freedom is always to be found
if we take the time to look.*

Day's End, Long Jetty, NSW

*In stillness
one begins to see
their true reflection.*

Tucked away in an inlet of Brisbane Water,
Hardys Bay retains the charm of a close-knit
waterside community. It's the sort of place where
everyone knows each other, and where the link
between the water and daily life remains strong.

THIS PAGE
Sunrise, Hardys Bay, NSW

NEXT PAGE
Terrigal Beach aerial, NSW

*This is courage in a man:
to bear unflinchingly
what heaven sends.*

*Norah Head Lighthouse – seen here across the bay
of Pebbly Beach – is one of the most distinctive
features of the Central Coast's northern reaches.
In this picture, sunrise heralds a brand new day
as the lighthouse farewells the final shadows of night.*

PREVIOUS PAGE
Pelicans, The Haven, Terrigal, NSW

THIS PAGE
Sunrise, Norah Head Lighthouse, NSW

*When you've seen beyond
yourself then you may find
peace of mind
is waiting there.*

*Still waters and a glorious sunrise coalesce
to form a picture perfect scene at this footbridge
in Budgewoi. The symbolism is strengthened
by a lone figure on the arc of the bridge,
gazing upon the water in quiet contemplation.*

THIS PAGE
Contemplation, Budgewoi, NSW

NEXT PAGE
Gosford aerial, NSW

*Change your thoughts
and you can change
your world!*

*The Central Coast features many beautiful rural
enclaves, with an abundance of delightful acreages
and small farms. At the close of summer
many of these places – like this one in Oak Road,
Matcham – burst into a riot of autumn colour.*

Autumn Leaves, Oak Road, Matcham, NSW

*The best way out
is always through.*

Glenworth Valley is one of Australia's great free-range
horse-riding facilities, where horses can be ridden
unsupervised through thousands of acres of beautiful
countryside. Taken just after daybreak,
this spectacular shot shows the horses crashing
through the creek during the daily round-up.

THIS PAGE
Roundup, Glenworth Valley, NSW

NEXT PAGE
Avoca Beach aerial, NSW

ANON

*A strong person
and a waterfall
always channel
their own path.*

*Less imposing than the main Somersby Falls
(see pages 4–5) these lower falls on the same creek
offer a scene of great tranquillity and tenderness.
Moss and lichen, boulders and melaleuca trees –
all combine to offset the gentle cascades of water.*

PREVIOUS PAGE
Sunrise, North Avoca, NSW

THIS PAGE
Floods Creek, Somersby, NSW

JOHN LENNON

Time you enjoy wasting,
was not wasted.

A blue sea, well protected by rocky reefs from ocean
swells, allures visitors to beautiful Bateau Bay Beach.
Its relative seclusion (down steep steps) and its
sheltered swimming areas make this beach ideal
for those families who discover it.

THIS PAGE
Bateau Bay, NSW

NEXT PAGE
Sheathers Wharf, Koolewong, NSW

First Light, Terrigal, NSW

DESTINATION CENTRAL COAST
First published 2007
Reprinted 2010 and 2011
by Panographs Publishing Pty Ltd
ABN 21 050 235 606
PO Box 3015 Wamberal
NSW 2260 Australia
Telephone +61 2 4367 6777
Email: panos@kenduncan.com

Panographs is a registered
trademark of the Ken Duncan
Group Pty Limited.
Photography and text
by Ken Duncan
©2007 Divine Guidance P/L
Designed by Good Catch Design
Reprographics by CFL Print Studio
Printed and bound in China

The National Library of Australia
Cataloguing-in-Publication entry:

Duncan, Ken
Destination Central Coast:
magnificent panoramic views.
ISBN 9780977573073.
1. Central Coast (N.S.W.) -
Description and travel - Pictorial
works. I. Title.
919.44200222

To view the range of Ken Duncan's
panoramic Limited Edition Prints
visit our Galleries:

- 414 The Entrance Road,
  Erina Heights, NSW
  Telephone +61 2 4367 6701

- 73 George Street, The Rocks,
  Sydney, NSW
  Telephone +61 2 9241 3460

- Level 1, 9 Star Circus,
  Harbour Town Shopping
  Centre, Docklands,
  Melbourne, Vic
  Telephone +61 3 9670 6971